The Bolshoi Ballet

A HELENE OBOLENSKY ENTERPRISES, INC., BOOK

The Bolshoi Ballet

Photographs by Judy Cameron

INTRODUCTION AND NOTES
BY WALTER TERRY

ICON EDITIONS
HARPER & ROW, PUBLISHERS
NEW YORK, EVANSTON, SAN FRANCISCO, LONDON

THE BOLSHOI BALLET. Introduction and notes copyright © 1975 by Harper
& Row, Publishers, Inc. Photographs copyright © by Judy Cameron and
Helene Obolensky Enterprises, Inc. All rights reserved. Printed in the United
States of America. No part of this book may be used or reproduced in any
manner whatsoever without written permission except in the case of brief
quotations embodied in critical articles and reviews. For information address
Harper & Row, Publishers, Inc., 10 East 53rd Street, New York, N.Y. 10022.
Published simultaneously in Canada by Fitzhenry & Whiteside Limited,
Toronto.

FIRST EDITION

ISBN: 0-06-430600-3 (cloth) 0-06-430063-3 (paper)

LIBRARY OF CONGRESS CATALOG CARD NUMBER: 74-25152

75 76 77 78 79 10 9 8 7 6 5 4 3 2 1

Contents

Introduction

BALLETS

PERFORMERS

INTRODUCTION

The birth of a nation and the birth of a ballet are, in their very separate areas of importance, *big* events. In 1976, we in the United States of America celebrate our bicentennial as a republic. In Moscow, the Bolshoi Ballet celebrates its two hundredth birthday. The word for *"big"* in Russian is *bolshoi* and it serves, 1976 as ballet itself does, as a link between two very different cultures.

Ballet, long before we knew the word *bolshoi,* provided a special connection between America and Russia. Indeed, for the first three decades of this century, the words "ballet" and "Russian" were inseparable in the minds of any American who professed an interest in ballet. Anna Pavlova, called "the immortal" and "the incomparable," re-awakened America's interest in ballet with her first visit and with her subsequent transcontinental tours over the years that followed. She, a product of the famed Maryinsky (now the Kirov) Theater in the city now called Leningrad, was not only the supreme symbol of Russian ballet for us, she *was* ballet itself.

Her colleague, Vaslav Nijinsky, the greatest male dancer of his era, visited us all too briefly in 1916, and reminded us that the almost forgotten *premier danseur* was a dazzling part of ballet.

Many of our ballet teachers, following the pioneering steps of Pavlova, came from Russia to put a Russian ballet stamp on the international technique of ballet. A little later, our eyes were opened by the choreographies of Fokine, Massine, and Balanchine, and by the dancing in the 1930s and 1940s of the great Alexandra Danilova and the famous "Baby Ballerinas"—the teenage Tamara Toumanova, Irina Baronova, and Tatiana Riabouchinska. But our eyes really opened in 1959 when Moscow's Bolshoi Ballet made its first trip to America.

The impact of the almost legendary Russian troupe on Americans was—well—*bolshoi.* Theater lobbies were crammed with people who had never seen ballet before, except on television or, perhaps, at Radio City Music Hall. Even America's ardent balletomanes

knew next to nothing about the Bolshoi. A handful had visited
the Soviet Union, an occasional photograph was published in a
dance magazine, and if you were a movie fan or researcher, you
might possibly have seen some old, old movies, mostly pre-World
War II, of Tatiana Semyonova as the "Queen of the Swans" in
a ballet excerpt. You might also have watched one of the most
breathtaking male dancers of the century, Vakhtang Chabukiani,
in a virtuosic excerpt from *Le Corsaire,* or caught a glimpse of the
fabulous Galina Ulanova and an even briefer glimpse of a startling
newcomer, Maya Plisetskaya. Oh, how we loved those bits and
pieces, black and white, poorly printed Bolshoi Ballet films that
reached us scratched and worn. And then came the real thing.

Audiences at New York's glittering old Metropolitan Opera
House and elsewhere throughout the country at last saw Ulanova
as Giselle and as Juliet, and knew instantly why she had been
called "the wonder of the world." She was almost fifty when we
saw her in Leonid Lavrovsky's staging of *Romeo and Juliet* but
she seemed hardly more than a child. It reminded me that the
great American actress Jane Cowl had answered those who
criticized her for playing Juliet when she was a mature woman
by saying that one had to be forty to know the wonder of
being fourteen.

And then, we saw Plisetskaya in *Swan Lake,* dancing the dual
role of Odette, the gentle "Queen of the Swans," and Odile, the
dazzling, evil "Black Swan" as she is often called. Plisetskaya
had the old Met shaking to the rafters with applause and cheers
for what most critics and fans considered to be one of the great
enactments of ballet. As Odette, her lyricism, the bird-like
quality of her tremulous arms, the mercurial movements of her
back and long neck entranced the viewer. And as the almost
harsh, bright and brazen Odile, she electrified that same audience
with dramatic malevolence and a virtuosity—dizzying turns, split
jumps, slashing kicks—seldom equalled.

Ulanova and Plisetskaya were the stars, but Americans came
soon to know the other dancers and to respond to the Bolshoi
style of ballet so different from our own. Our Russian teachers

had come from Leningrad where the ballet school was characterized by great elegance, but these Bolshoi dancers were Muscovites with a broader manner of dancing ballet, with a quality of physical daring that saw the men lift the girls over their heads, using only one arm, and the girls themselves flung, sometimes horizontally, through space to be caught with split-second timing by a seemingly insouciant male.

Small wonder that American ballet dancers rushed from Bolshoi performances to their own studios to try their skills at one-armed lifts and perilous hurtlings. The Bolshoi dancers also visited our ballet performances to see American-style ballet and were equally fascinated. The cultural exchange, with ballet as the commodity, was working.

Friends in dance for more than a decade, our two countries will be busy with 1976 festivities. In the U.S.S.R., celebrating will be focused upon Moscow, for it was in 1773 that the trustees of the Moscow Orphanage established ballet classes for its young charges who, by 1776, were ready to give their first public performance outside the orphanage. They danced in the Petrovsky Theater, the site of today's vast Bolshoi Theater.

National fame did not come at once. In fact, for almost two centuries ballet in Moscow took second place to the ballet in St. Petersburg, because that was the imperial capitol until the Revolution. Although the Czar and the court gave special support to the great Maryinsky Theater (now the Kirov) and the Russian Imperial Ballet that was housed there, the Imperial Ballet in Moscow was by no means neglected. Marius Petipa, master choreographer of Russia's unmatched classical ballet, staged his brilliant *Don Quixote*—still a Bolshoi trademark—at the Bolshoi; and some may have forgotten that Tchaikovsky's *Swan Lake* had its initial production in Moscow.

For almost a century, great Russian stars have brought Bolshoi-brand Russian ballet to the West. Among them have been Mikhail Mordkin, Pavlova's dashing and virile partner, and Leonide Massine whose choreography, ranging from his historic "symphonic ballets" (among them *Rouge et Noir,* set to the Shostakovitch Symphony No. 1) to the perennially popular *Le Beau Danube* and *Gaîté Parisienne,* enriched the theater of the twentieth century.

When the capitol moved to Moscow, the Bolshoi Ballet reached the peak it now holds. Long before this time, however, it had established its own Bolshoi style, not only *big* but also *grand* (another meaning of *bolshoi)* and—yes—flamboyant.

Today there are close to fifty state ballet companies in the Soviet Union and there are, very probably, more than a million ballet students in the U.S.S.R. But with ballet a major enterprise throughout the Soviet Union, the biggest troupe of all—it numbers a minimum of two hundred and fifty dancers, backed up with hundreds of students from the Bolshoi Ballet Theater School—is the Bolshoi Ballet itself. And, as it celebrates its artistic bicentennial, another definition of the word *bolshoi* may well be pertinent. That definition goes beyond *big* and *grand.* . . . for *Bolshoi,* in a very special sense, also signifies *Great.*

Walter Terry

In the following ballets
different dancers are portrayed
in the principal roles.

Spartacus

Ballet in 3 acts and 12 scenes
Book: Nikolai Volkov and Yuri Grigorovich, after an event in Roman history
Music: Aram Khachaturian
Choreography: Yuri Grigorovich
Scenery and Costumes: Simon Virzaladze
First Bolshoi Performance: The Bolshoi Theater, Moscow
April 1968
First Bolshoi Performance in the United States: New York, April 1975

Maris Liepa, Act I

Vladimir Vasiliev, Act I

Vladimir Vasiliev, Act I

Vladimir Vasiliev and Ekaterina Maximova, Act I

Natalia Bessmertnova and Mikhail Lavrovsky, Act I

Natalia Bessmertnova and Mikhail Lavrovsky, Act I

Ekaterina Maximova, Act I

Vladimir Vasiliev and Ekaterina Maximova, Act I

Vladimir Vasiliev, Act I

Vladimir Vasiliev, Act II

Maris Liepa, Act II

Maris Liepa, Act II

Maris Liepa and Nina Timofeyeva, Act II

Maris Liepa, Act II

Vladimir Vasiliev, Act II

Vladimir Vasiliev, Act II

Vladimir Vasiliev, Act II

Vladimir Vasiliev, Act III

Vladimir Vasiliev, Act III

Vladimir Vasiliev, Act III

Mikhail Lavrovsky and Natalia Bessmertnova, Act III

Mikhail Lavrovsky and Natalia Bessmertnova, Act III

Giselle

Ballet in 2 acts
Book: Théophile Gautier and Vernoy de St Georges
Music: Adolphe Adam
Choreography: Jean Coralli, Jules Perrot, Marius Petipa
First Bolshoi Performance: The Bolshoi Theater, Moscow
                              November 1843
Revised Production: Leonid Lavrovsky, 1944
Scenery and Costumes: Nikolai Volkov
First Bolshoi Performance in the United States: New York, April 1959

Ekaterina Maximova, Act I

Natalia Bessmertnova, Act I

Vladimir Vasiliev and Ekaterina Maximova, Act I

Ekaterina Maximova and Maris Liepa, Act I

Nina Timofeyeva, Act I

Vladimir Vasiliev, Act I

Ekaterina Maximova, Act I

Ekaterina Maximova, Act I

Ekaterina Maximova, Act I

Natalia Bessmertnova, Act II

Natalia Bessmertnova, Act II

Vladimir Vasiliev, Act II

Ekaterina Maximova and Vladimir Vasiliev, Act II

Ekaterina Maximova and Vladimir Vasiliev, Act II

Natalia Bessmertnova, Act II

Mikhail Lavrovsky and Natalia Bessmertnova, Act II

Ludmilla Semenyaka and Nicolai Fadeyechev, Act II

Don Quixote

Ballet in 4 acts and 8 scenes
Book: After the novel by Miguel de Cervantes
Music: Leon Minkus
Choreography: Marius Petipa
First Bolshoi Performance: The Bolshoi Theater, Moscow
December 1869
Revised Production: Aleksandr Gorsky and Rostislav Zakharov
Scenery and Costumes: Vadim Rindin
First Bolshoi Performance in the United States: New York, April 1966

Natalia Bessmertnova, Act I

Ekaterina Maximova and Vladimir Vasiliev, Act I

Ekaterina Maximova and Vladimir Vasiliev, Act I

Ekaterina Maximova, Act I

Ekaterina Maximova, Act I

Ekaterina Maximova and Rimma Karelskaya, Act II

Vladimir Vasiliev and Ekaterina Maximova, Act II

Ekaterina Maximova, Act II

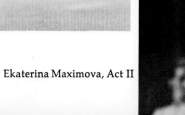

Ekaterina Maximova, Act II

Vladimir Vasiliev and Ekaterina Maximova, Act III

Vladimir Vasiliev and Ekaterina Maximova, Act III

Vladimir Vasiliev, Act III

Vladimir Vasiliev and Ekaterina Maximova, curtain call

Swan Lake

Ballet in 4 acts
Book: Vladimir Begitchev and Vasily Geltzer
Music: Pyotr Ilyich Tchaikovsky
Choreography: Julius Reisinger
First Bolshoi Performance: The Bolshoi Theater, Moscow
                                February 1877
            Revised: Marius Petipa and Lev Ivanov
                    Maryinsky Theater, St. Petersburg
                    January 1895
Revised Production: Yuri Grigorovich, 1970
Scenery and Costumes: Simon Virzaladze
First Bolshoi Performance in the United States: New York, April 1959

Maya Plisetskaya, Act II

Maya Plisetskaya, Act II

Alexander Bogatyrev and Natalia Bessmertnova, Act II

Natalia Bessmertnova, Act II

Alexander Godounov and Maya Plisetskaya, Act II

Alexander Bogatyrev and Natalia Bessmertnova, Act III

Tatyana Golikova and Alexander Bogatyrev, Act III

Alexander Bogatyrev and Ludmilla Semenyaka, Act III

Natalia Bessmertnova and Alexander Bogatyrev, Act IV

Natalia Bessmertnova, curtain call

Romeo and Juliet

Ballet in 3 acts and 13 scenes, with prologue and epilogue
Book: Leonid Lavrovsky and Sergei Prokofiev, after Shakespeare
Music: Sergei Prokofiev
Choreography: Leonid Lavrovsky
Scenery and Costumes: Pyotr Williams
First Bolshoi Performance: The Bolshoi Theater, Moscow
December 1946
First Bolshoi Performance in the United States: New York, April 1959

Natalia Bessmertnova, Act I

Ekaterina Maximova, Act I

Ekaterina Maximova, Act I

Natalia Bessmertnova and Vladimir Vasiliev, Act I

Natalia Bessmertnova and Vladimir Vasiliev, Act I

Natalia Bessmertnova and Vladimir Vasiliev, Act I

Natalia Bessmertnova and Mikhail Gabovich, Act I

Natalia Bessmertnova and Mikhail Gabovich, Act I

Vladimir Vasiliev and Ekaterina Maximova, Act I

Vladimir Vasiliev and Ekaterina Maximova, Act I

Natalia Bessmertnova and Mikhail Gabovich, Act II

Natalia Bessmertnova and Mikhail Gabovich, Act II

Mikhail Tzvin, Act II

Vladimir Levashev and Vladimir Vasiliev, Act II

Mikhail Tzvin, Act II

Ekaterina Maximova and Vladimir Vasiliev, Act III

Natalia Bessmertnova and Vladimir Vasiliev, Act III

Natalia Bessmertnova and Mikhail Lavrovsky, Act III

Natalia Bessmertnova and Mikhail Lavrovsky, Act III

Natalia Bessmertnova, Act III

Ekaterina Maximova, Act III

Natalia Bessmertnova
and Vladimir Vasiliev, Act III

Natalia Bessmertnova and Mikhail Lavrovsky, Act III

Natalia Bessmertnova, Act III

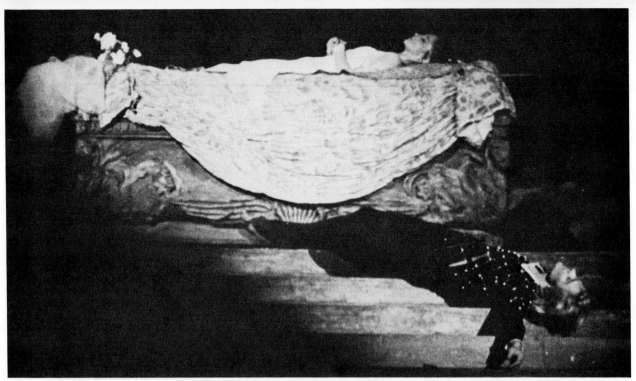

Vladimir Vasiliev and Natalia Bessmertnova, Act III

Vladimir Vasiliev and Natalia Bessmertnova, Act III

Natalia Bessmertnova and Mikhail Gabovich, Act III

The Sleeping Beauty

Ballet in 3 acts and 5 scenes, with prologue
Book: After the fairy tale by Charles Perrault
Music: Pyotr Ilyich Tchaikovsky
Choreography: Marius Petipa
First Bolshoi Performance: The Bolshoi Theater, Moscow
                                    January 1899
Revised Production: Yuri Grigorovich, 1973
Scenery and Costumes: Simon Virzaladze
First Bolshoi Performance in the United States: New York, April 1975

Nina Sorokina, Act I

Ekaterina Maximova, Act I

Nina Sorokina, Act I

Nina Sorokina, Act I

Ekaterina Maximova, Act I

Alexander Bogatyrev and Ekaterina Maximova, Act II

Marina Kondratyeva and Maris Liepa, Act III

Ekaterina Maximova and Alexander Bogatyrev, Act III

Ekaterina Maximova and Alexander Bogatyrev, Act III

MAYA PLISETSKAYA

Maya Plisetskaya is currently Russia's only *prima ballerina assoluta,* succeeding to that highest rank in all ballet upon the retirement of the great Galina Ulanova. Indeed, the world's only other *assoluta* (which means "absolute") is England's Dame Margot Fonteyn. As a child Maya was precocious and learned her ballet assignments so quickly that her teachers were hard put to keep her interested. A little later, she went directly from the Bolshoi school into the company as a soloist, completely skipping the customary years of dancing in the corps de ballet.

Her technique even in maturity is prodigious and her versatility remarkable. Not only did she captivate the American public in the full-length *Swan Lake* but she moved them to tears as another swan, *The Dying Swan* (the miniature solo immortalized by Pavlova) in which the rippling of her arms evoked gasps of wonderment (and often as many as three encores!). Her coquettish Kitri in *Don Quixote* is irresistible; and in the title role of her favorite ballet, *Carmen Suite,* she is both fierce and fiery, a figure who faces death with exultant vitality. With *Anna Karenina,* she emerges a dancer-actress and also the choreographer of her first ballet. In Maris Liepa she has a costar of stunning virtuosity and experience, and in young Alexander Godounov she has a striking partner who is a worthy attendant of the Bolshoi's *prima ballerina assoluta.*

As Carmen in *Carmen Suite*

As Kitri with Maris Liepa as Basilio in *Don Quixote*

As Anna Karénina with Maris Liepa as Vronsky in *Anna Karenina*

As Anna Karenina in *Anna Karenina*

As Carmen in *Carmen Suite*

As Carmen with Alexander Godounov as Don José in *Carmen Suite*

As Odette with Nicolai Fadeyechev as Siegfried in *Swan Lake*

As Odette in *Swan Lake* (curtain call)

VLADIMIR VASILIEV

Vladimir Vasiliev comes to us at the peak of his powers as one of the great *premiers danseurs* of our era. Americans cheered him as a phenomenon when he first danced in the United States in 1959 as the youth in Yuri Grigorovich's *The Stone Flower*. Grigorovich, the Soviet Union's finest choreographer and the Bolshoi Ballet's artistic director, has restaged classical ballets with Vasiliev in mind for principal roles and he has even created major works focusing upon this young artist's special talents. *Spartacus,* a ballet that went through several unsuccessful versions until Grigorovich himself choreographed it into a contemporary masterwork, has become a special showcase for Vasiliev. And in the new *Ivan the Terrible,* Grigorovich has provided the mature but still youthful (at thirty-five) star with yet another ballet to add to a roster of successes.

Frequently, Vasiliev dances with his ballerina-wife, Ekaterina Maximova, together making one of the great ballet duos of the day. Their *Don Quixote,* among the classics, is a favorite with audiences at home and abroad. His honors are many; among them have been the Nijinsky Prize (Paris 1964), the prestigious gold medal at the International Ballet Competition (Varna, Bulgaria, 1964), and the coveted Lenin Prize (1970).

As Spartacus in *Spartacus*

As Basilio in *Don Quixote*

As Basilio in *Don Quixote*

With Maya Plisetskaya (in class)

As Ivan with Natalia Bessmertnova as Anastasia
in *Ivan the Terrible* (rehearsal)

As Ivan in *Ivan the Terrible* (rehearsal)

As Ivan in *Ivan the Terrible* (rehearsal)

NATALIA BESSMERTNOVA

Natalia Bessmertnova has that very special ballerina quality that is often described as "mystique." Paradoxically, that means a quality that cannot be described at all! What one senses in an artist such as Bessmertnova is a mysterious power that draws the viewers' attention to her by her mere presence on stage, whether she is dancing or standing immobile. Perhaps this very special quality is a result of her total identification with dancing —she began at four—and her unending dedication to it.

Bessmertnova, beautiful to behold simply when her exceptionally lovely arms are etched in space and her body in anticipatory repose, is also a superb virtuoso. Her "Black Swan" is thrilling as a bravura display, but in a ballet such as *Giselle*, a favorite with her public, she combines her technical prowess with a portrayal of the doomed heroine that touches the heart. She is, of course, a lovely Juliet and an entrancing Sugar Plum Fairy (in *Nutcracker*), and when it comes to *The Dying Swan*, she has her own highly personal interpretation of a role that challenges every ballerina but thwarts most. America, as well as her native Russia, has its legion of Bessmertnova fans who sigh over her and cheer for her in the ballet classics, and eagerly await her dancing in her famous husband's newest creation, Grigorovich's *Ivan the Terrible*.

As Phrygie in *Spartacus*

In *Flower Festival* Pas de Deux

As Macha with Vladimir Vasiliev as the Prince
in *Nutcracker*

As Odette in *Swan Lake*

As Odette in *Swan Lake*

EKATERINA MAXIMOVA

Ekaterina Maximova is the very special protégée of the legendary Galina Ulanova, for Mme. Ulanova has coached her not only in roles that she herself immortalized but also in new parts that **reveal** Maximova's unique qualities as a superb technician and a personality that is all sunshine and radiance in romantic roles and appealing sadness in tragedies.

Her "line," that special balletic quality that describes the perfection of a body from toe to fingertips, from arched foot to arched neck as it is silhouetted in space, is one of her special attributes. But she is also noted for her soaring leg extensions, her lightness of step, and balances on *pointe* that gleefully defy gravity.

Maximova is an accomplished actress-dancer; in her most popular role, her humor is infectious as Kitri in *Don Quixote*—and also breathtaking is her rocket-like *grand jeté*; her sweetness and elegance admirable in *The Nutcracker*; and her interpretation of the tragic Giselle (in which she was directed by the incomparable Ulanova) an unforgettable portrait in dance.

Her most dashing partner is very often her husband, Vladimir Vasiliev.

In class

As Cinderella in *Cinderella*

As Cinderella in *Cinderella*

In *Melody*

With Vladimir Vasiliev in *Nutcracker* (curtain call)

MIKHAIL LAVROVSKY

Mikhail Lavrovsky bears a distinguished name to which he has added further distinction. His father, Leonid Lavrovsky, was one of Russia's great choreographers; the son is one of Russia's great dancers. Appropriately, one of his finest achievements is his Romeo in his father's celebrated choreographic setting of the great Shakespearean love story.

In an old classic, *Giselle*, he and Bessmertnova are among the most poignant and passionate Albrechts and Giselles of our day. And in the new choreography of the old *Nutcracker*, his role of the Prince was created for him by his father's successor as the U.S.S.R.'s foremost choreographer, Yuri Grigorovich, whose *Spartacus* also provides him with a major part. Lavrovsky and Vasiliev, both *premiers danseurs* of uncommon skills, are quite different from each other. Vasiliev is blond, open of manner and, when the part permits, lightly humorous. Lavrovsky is dark of hair and dark of mien and mood. He is slender, yet muscled as a classical Greek athlete. There is ardor just under his sometimes somber look and poetry of gesture even in movements demanding great strength. His wife is a ballerina, Ludmilla Semenyaka, but he partners many a star from the veteran Struchkova through Maximova, Timofeyeva and Sorokina to Bessmertnova.

In 1965, he won the gold medal at the International Ballet Competition at Varna, Bulgaria, and was awarded the Lenin Prize in 1970.

As Spartacus in *Spartacus*

As Spartacus with Natalia Bessmertnova as Phrygie
in *Spartacus*

As Spartacus with Natalia Bessmertnova as Phrygie
in *Spartacus*

As Spartacus in *Spartacus*

As Spartacus with Natalia Bessmertnova as Phrygie
in *Spartacus* (curtain call)

Nina Sorokina and Yuri Vladimirov are the Bolshoi's most spectacular husband-and-wife team and one of their most spectacular showpieces is the always-encored pas de deux from *Flames of Paris*. Here, Sorokina spins at an incredible speed or hops with steel-like lightness on *pointe* while Vladimirov, a dancing cosmonaut, soars heavenward while rotating in space performing dazzling steps that very probably have no name in ballet books. In modern ballet style, for which there is no universal terminology, Vladimirov accomplishes unbelievable feats of skill in a 1965 staging (by Vladimir Vasiliov and his wife Natalia Kasatkina) of Stravinsky's *Rite of Spring*, with Sorokina as the Young Girl. The two have yet another display piece for themselves in the popular *Diana and Actaeon* pas de deux.

Sorokina, a protégée of one of the very great ballerinas of the past, Marina Semyonova, was a gold medalist at the International Ballet Competition in Varna, Bulgaria, in 1966. The same year, Vladimirov won the gold medal for the men.

The two, of course, dance separately with other stars of the Bolshoi, but when they dance together there is a special excitement on stage because they manage to suggest an air of competition while displaying absolute perfection as a "team."

Nina Sorokina as Diana with Yuri Vladimirov
as Actaeon in *Diana and Actaeon*

Yuri Vladimirov as Spartacus in *Spartacus*

Nina Sorokina as Macha in *Nutcracker*

Yuri Vladimirov as Ivan with Natalia Bessmertnova as Anastasia
in *Ivan the Terrible* (rehearsal)

Yuri Vladimirov as Ivan with Natalia Bessmertnova as Anastasia
in *Ivan the Terrible* (rehearsal)

VLADIMIR LEVASHEV

Vladimir Levashev is not the fairy-tale prince of classical
ballet. He is more likely to be a king or a villain or a magician.
He is, indeed, that artist most important to story-ballets, the
character dancer, the actor, the mime. Levashev's roles range from
the dashing, doomed Mercutio in *Romeo and Juliet* to the evil
Bailiff in *The Stone Flower*, from the Czar in *The Humpbacked
Horse* to one of the exuberant Spanish, Polish, or Hungarian
dancers in classical ballet's national dances divertissements.

He is the wildly passionate Khan in *The Fountain of Bakhchisarai*,
as well as the malevolent magician von Rothbart (perhaps his
greatest acting role) in *Swan Lake*.

Levashev, the Bolshoi's great character dancer, has come a
long way since his childhood debut as an actor-dancer—he was
the prancing, strutting rooster in a school play!

As Drosselmeyer with Nina Sorokina as Macha
in *Nutcracker*

As the Tsar with Maya Plisetskaya as the Tsar Maiden
in *The Humbacked Horse*

As Rothbart in *Swan Lake*

NINA TIMOFEYEVA

Nina Timofeyeva is a name that rolls as smoothly off the tongue as her dancing caresses the stage. As a child prodigy when she was barely seven, she startled family and friends with her natural, untutored dancing, and when still a teenage student, she delighted audiences with her accomplishments in one of the ballerina's most difficult assignments, *La Bayadère*.

She began her career, as did her famous teacher Galina Ulanova, at the Kirov in Leningrad, onetime headquarters of the Russian Imperial Ballet. At the Bolshoi, whenever she adds a new role to her immense repertory, Mme. Ulanova is there to guide her.

Timofeyeva's range as an artist, both as interpreter and virtuosa, is prodigious. She electrified American audiences first in *Swan Lake* in 1959 (her dazzling sequence of thirty-two *fouettés* in Act III were the first we had seen done by a Soviet star), but her ballets also include *Legend of Love*, *Laurencia* (spectacular), *Chopiniana* (which we know as the lovely and lyrical *Les Sylphides*), the exuberant *Don Quixote*, the lusty Armenian-flavored *Gayané*, the classical *The Sleeping Beauty*, *Romeo and Juliet*, *Giselle* (from the Romantic Age of Ballet), *Spartacus* (a contemporary ballet) and, well, almost any ballet you care to name.

As Giselle in *Giselle*

As Aegina with Maris Liepa as Crassus in *Spartacus*

As Aegina in *Spartacus*

As Aegina in *Spartacus*

Maris Liepa and Marina Kondratieva are admired by Americans as a duo in both *Giselle* and *Les Sylphides* and separately in any of a number of Bolshoi productions.

Liepa is quite simply "remarkable." His versatility in every area of dance fairly takes one's breath away, for he is an accomplished *premier danseur* in classical roles, a towering figure of smashing virility in *Spartacus* (Londoners thought of him as "the Laurence Olivier of the dance"), an elusive dream-figure in Fokine's *Le Spectre de la Rose* (he is the U.S.S.R.'s most knowledgeable and successful interpreter of the Fokine style in ballet), an actor in Russian movies, a choreographer for Soviet television, an experimenter with avant-garde dance forms, a recitalist (he has given an all-Liepa starring program to capacity audiences in Moscow), and a fluent conversationalist in English as well as in Russian. In 1969, he was named a People's Artist of the U.S.S.R. and awarded the Lenin Prize.

Kondratieva has won her following not only through the beauty of her dancing but also for her broad, split leap which comes like an exclamation point at the end of a sentence in dance movement.

Maris Liepa with Marina Kondratieva
in *Chopiniana (Les Sylphides)*

Maris Liepa as Crassus in *Spartacus*

Maris Liepa as Crassus in *Spartacus*

Marina Kondratieva as Giselle in *Giselle*

On the French Riviera

LUDMILLA SEMENYAKA

Ludmilla Semenyaka is a Leningrad-trained dancer, a product
of the St. Petersburg tradition that produced Pavlova, Karsavina,
Nijinsky, and many of the Russian ballet greats of the past.
Upon leaving the Kirov in 1972, she joined the Bolshoi Ballet
after winning a prize in the International Moscow Ballet
Competition. Prizes are not unknown to the family; her husband,
Mikhail Lavrovsky had won his gold medal seven years earlier
at the famed Varna competition. Her roles in *Swan Lake,
Giselle, Nutcracker, Legend of Love,* and other ballets are
prepared under the supervision of Ulanova.

She was seen briefly in America in 1973 when she danced with
a touring unit of the Bolshoi Ballet.

As Odette in *Swan Lake*

As Giselle in *Giselle*

As Giselle in *Giselle*

As Shirine with Alexander Bogatyrev
in *Legend of Love*

In *Legend of Love*

As Macha with Vyacheslav Gordeyev as the Prince
in *Nutcracker*

With Galina Ulanova (rehearsal)

NADESHDA PAVLOVA AND
VYACHESLAV GORDEYEV

Nadeshda Pavlova and Vyacheslav Gordeyev were winners in
the All-Soviet Ballet Competition in Moscow in 1972. In 1973,
these teenagers, in company with such stars as Struchkova and
Liepa, made their New York debut with a unit of the Bolshoi
Ballet in company with students from the Bolshoi Ballet
Theater Academy.

The name "Pavlova" evokes an air of magic, and the young
Nadeshda did honor to the earlier (Anna) Pavlova by dancing
not only with technical perfection but with style and grace.
American audiences were quick to hail this girl from Perm (a
ballet center of growing importance in the U.S.S.R.) and to ask to
see more of her—in major ballets—than the short divertissements
of the 1973 tour permitted.

Gordeyev, her male counterpart, won himself an instant
following with a technical prowess unexpected in the unheralded
newcomer. In his twenties, Gordeyev is already dancing leads
in *Spartacus* and *Don Quixote* and is paired often with Pavlova,
the youngest soloist of the Bolshoi Ballet, in *Nutcracker*.

Nadia Pavlova as Macha with Vyacheslav Gordeyev as

Nadia Pavlova as Macha with Vyacheslav Gordeyev as
the Prince in *Nutcracker*

Nadia Pavlova as Macha with Vyacheslav Gordeyev as
the Prince in *Nutcracker*

In class with Gordeyev

Before performance

As Macha in *Nutcracker*

As Macha in *Nutcracker*

RAISA STRUCHKOVA

Raisa Struchkova, a veteran Bolshoi ballerina (she was born
in 1925), has long been as popular abroad as in her homeland.
On the Bolshoi Ballet's first trip to America in 1959, she alternated
with Galina Ulanova in *Romeo and Juliet*; and although Ulanova
was hailed as the greatest of ballet's Juliets, Struchkova, with
her own interpretation and high artistry, earned lavish praise
from press and public who recognized in her not only a
ballerina but a *prima ballerina*. In addition to her skills as an
actress-dancer in *Romeo and Juliet, Cinderella,* and other
full-length ballets, she is equally at home in those short
showpieces that require Bolshoi dancers to electrify audiences
in a matter of minutes with explosions of virtuosity and
split-second timings realized with an ever-alert partner in
perilous leaps, falls, and catches. One such partner is the
ballerina's husband, Alexander Lapauri.

Movie buffs around the world are familiar with a full-length
film, *Cinderella,* starring Struchkova.

As Cinderella in *Cinderella* (curtain call)

As Cinderella in *Cinderella*

As Cinderella in *Cinderella*

As Cinderella in *Cinderella*

NICOLAI FADEYECHEV

Nicolai Fadeyechev has long been the ballerina's dream of a perfect cavalier, for he is attentive yet unobtrusive, presenting the female star for the audience to admire. He is physically strong as a partner, yet his romantic air gives him the quality of effortlessness. Thus, with this romantic air and his acting skills, he makes a splendid Albrecht in *Giselle,* a handsome Prince in *The Sleeping Beauty,* a tormented Siegfried in *Swan Lake* and, most recently, the doomed Don José in *Carmen Suite* in which he dances, as he has done over the years in many ballets, with Plisetskaya.

His easy style sometimes makes audiences forget that he is something more than an admirable partner and thus, when he comes to his solo variation close to the end of *Giselle,* viewers are surprised to see him do the leaps and the intricate leg-beats, the swift multiple turns that they normally associate with more bravura-style dancers.

His high estate as a cavalier is attested to by the fact that Ulanova chose him to dance with her in a movie of *Giselle* and Plisetskaya selected him for her partner in a film of *Swan Lake.* What greater praise could a gentleman of the ballet receive!

As Siegfried in *Swan Lake*

As Albrecht with Ludmilla Semenyaka as Giselle in *Giselle*

As Albrecht with Ludmilla Semenyaka as Giselle in *Giselle*

ALEXANDER GODOUNOV

Alexander Godounov, like his brilliant senior in the Bolshoi,
Maris Liepa, is blond, virile, dashing, versatile, and
Latvian-born (Riga).

He made his debut—and a highly successful one it was—with
Bessmertnova in *Swan Lake* in 1971. Soon, he became a favorite
of the fiery Plisetskaya, and has danced with her not only
in *Swan Lake* but in such exclusive Plisetskaya vehicles as
Carmen Suite, in which he is a passionate Don José, in her own
Anna Karenina, which she choreographed, and in *La Rose Malade,*
especially choreographed for her by France's Roland Petit.

Godounov's principal teacher is one of the great ballet masters
of the Soviet Union and Plisetskaya's uncle, Asaf Messerer.

Godounov with his long blond hair, powerful body, and
dynamic presence is a great favorite with most young
balletomanes not only in the U.S.S.R. but also in the United States.

In Disneyland, Anaheim, California

With Maya Plisetskaya in *La Rose Malade*

In class

BORIS AKIMOV

Boris Akimov is a pupil of one of the great Bolshoi stars,
Maris Liepa, who is known for his teaching skill as well as for
his performing artistry. Perhaps it was from Liepa that Akimov
learned the importance of versatility and the need to master
characterization as well as technique. For in *Swan Lake* he has
danced both the role of the handsome hero, the Prince, and
the evil magician, Rothbart.

An injury kept him off stage for almost two years, but he busied
himself teaching the junior soloists of the Bolshoi and returned,
his technical skills unimpaired, to dance not only *Swan Lake* but
also *Spartacus* and the buoyant Danish showpiece in the
romantic style of the nineteenth-century August Bournonville,
the pas de deux from *Flower Festival at Genzano.*

As Siegfried in *Swan Lake*

In *Flower Festival*

In *Flower Festival*

As Crassus in *Spartacus*

ALEXANDER BOGATYREV

Alexander Bogatyrev seems to be the heir of the now
retiring Fadeyechev in the field of classical ballet. The
twenty-five-year-old native of Estonia, like Fadeyechev, makes
an ideal prince, for he is elegant of step and deportment and a
gallant cavalier for the ballerina. As he moves into position as the
Bolshoi's most classical male dancer—perhaps a *premier danseur
noble* to be—he is paired with the superb Bessmertnova in
such ballets as *Giselle* and with other ballerinas in assignments
requiring both solo prowess and partnering skill.

As Albrecht with Natalia Bessmertnova as Giselle in *Giselle*

As Siegfried in *Swan Lake* Pas de Trois with Irina Prokofieva
and Natasha Filipova

As Siegfried with Natalia Bessmertnova as Odette in *Swan Lake*

YURI GRIGOROVICH

Yuri Grigorovich, a product of the Kirov Ballet in Leningrad, is not only the artistic director of the Bolshoi Ballet but also Russia's most distinguished and successful choreographer. Even as a student and later as a *demi-caractère* soloist with the Kirov, he disclosed strong choreographic leanings and, in 1957, his first major work, a wholly new staging of the Prokofiev *The Stone Flower* (originally with choreography by Lavrovsky), was produced with resounding success. The ballet *Spartacus*, which went through several unsatisfactory versions, emerged triumphant in his new and original 1968 staging. His new stagings of the traditional classics, *The Nutcracker* among them, have won international praise. A new *The Sleeping Beauty* is his and his own *Legend of Love* (1962) is a Soviet favorite. His newest creation, one that he has worked on for years and that is of major importance to him personally, is *Ivan the Terrible*. For the Bolshoi Ballet, Yuri Grigorovich, director-choreographer, is as much a star as are his glittering dancers.

216